How to Get What You Want Out of Life

I0439289

Caution! Be really careful about what you want because what you desire may not be all it appears to be. This is more than sage advice. It is critical that you set prudent goals because you are very likely to achieve them.

I once had a goal of going horseback riding on the Continental Divide. The goal was set and objectives were met. I overcame tremendous adversity and finally I was seated on horse on a mountain in the dead of winter near Gallup New Mexico. The scenery was spectacular and I was living the dream! The dream soon turned a nightmare for me because I did do my homework. I had never even touched a horse and never taken a lesson. The worst part was that an old spinal injury sent zaps of nerve pain up my spine ever time the horse took a step. I and the horse were a little stressed out that day and eventually ten minutes into my adventure I had to call it off. Be careful what your goals are. You might not like the results!

There are plenty of books that describe techniques for attracting money and a spouse. This book is about how to get everything else. This little book will teach you the secrets to setting goals and really programming your mind so that you will naturally do the things you need to do in order to get what you want. While there are no guarantees in life; you can stack the odds in your favor. You can achieve seemly impossible things in your life by using good strategy and self-discipline.

I will use examples from my life and close friends to illustrate how these powerful principles work. I have changed their names and identifying characteristics. May you use these principles in a responsible manner!

Principle #1 A goal has to be concrete.

If you ask a teenager what they want when they get older. Many will say, "I want a job, house, and a car." This answer is really a non-answer because it is so vague it tells you almost nothing. In all likelihood unless this teen gets serious, they will live at home and drift for some time in the sea of life. Eventually they may take up some kind of work, live somewhere else and drive something. Millions of families struggle with the failure to launch children. It can get really ugly as they get older. See "How to Make Your Kid Move Out" by James Nugent at Amazon.com

Be that as it may, all of us need to make our personal goals concrete if we want to seize control of our lives. So here are some ways to make your goals real.

-See it and say it.

Start to visualize and talk about it with supportive people. Take ten whole seconds a day or several times a day to imagine your goal and what it would be like. Picture in your mind achieving the goal.

I wanted to go to graduate school and had no money for: food, shelter or tuition. The thing I did right was focus on the goal. If I focused on the problems I would have been overwhelmed and never gone. In fact it took two graduate school attempts before I made it. In the first attempt I was living in subfreezing temperatures and got frostbite on my left hand. In second attempt I was in a slightly milder climate and I had developed resources and skills that helped me through it all.

The idea is that if you can imagine success and you talk about achievement of your goal it can become real.

One of the big things I failed to do in my first attempt at graduate student was talk about my goal. I kept it to myself. I missed out on emotional and practical support because I didn't let it be known that I was going to go to graduate school. It turned out that a relative lived in the town where I was going and had a part time job to give me. I didn't know about this because I was very private about the whole thing.

When we talk about something it becomes a plausible reality. People respond to it and you as if it were real. People have ideas and will share resources with us.

In the year before I first went to graduate school I told no one. This ended up causing great stress between me and my girlfriend. She actually exploded at me and said, "Look at yourself! Nothing has changed in 6 months. You have not done anything."

Actually I had taken a job as a life guard and was at the pool 30 hours a week thinking about the most important decision of my life. What was I was going to study in graduate school? When she yelled at me, I was one day away from making the critical decision and right after that I decided to also leave her . We did have issues that went beyond my hesitance to communicate.

However if I had talked about graduate school she would have had an opportunity to at least respond to the idea. If she was supportive I would have had another motivation to succeed. As it was, I left December 31 in the winter cold on an unheated sailboat and sailed to graduate school with little food or money and 2 ½ years of study to do. It didn't work out.

However two years later I tried it again, 120 miles south. It did work out! In the two years between the first and second attempt; I had learned a lot about goal setting, success and achievement. The lessons from graduate school and the next quarter century of living life to the fullest; resulted in the formulation of my principals for success and this little book.

Talking About your Goals

As soon I registered in school (the second time) I talked about it and referred to myself as Master's Degree student or a Master's Candidate. When I started to write books I referred to myself as an author for Amazon.com. When I studied weather and water sampling I called myself a Citizen Scientist. When I started to study Spanish in order to become a Spanish teacher I referred to myself as a Spanish Teacher in training and I traveled to Spanish speaking countries three times per year. When I was learning to fly small planes, I hung out with pilots at the airport and called myself a student private pilot. People feel much more comfortable and can be much more supportive when they know who you are and why you are in there world.

All of these things were necessary if I was going to make my goals real to me and achieve them. When people treat you seriously about your goals; you feel like they are coming true. When you think and feel good about your goals, you are far more likely to achieve them. Fear of failure is a waste of energy. You will either achieve your goal or not. Worry just makes it less likely you will fail.

Principle #2 Make the goal as tangible as possible.

In order to really see your goal it will help if you have artifacts that will remind you of your goal. Get a t-shirt or a poster for your wall. At every opportunity you want to beS reminded of your goal. Gather little tokens or key chains that work to make your goal real to you. Start to dress like the people who do your goal. When I wanted to become a counselor I dressed like a counselor. When I did a stint as a commercial diver I played the part. When I was an instructor at the Community College I even worn glasses to read on my nose. It is more than role playing it is method acting. It is programing, yourself, to believe. If you believe, other people will believe.

It is possible to irritate or even aggravate other people if you are too assertive or loud about your goals. Do not be a braggart but when people draw you out with a question be sure to tell them what you are up to. On the other hand if you are evasive they will just be suspicious of your activities and motivations, and your veracity.

Some people want to just be themselves. Well guess what? You can be yourself and maybe nobody else will believe in you. Without supportive people it is less likely you will achieve your goal.

I once was a mentor for a young professional in his early twenties. He was quite possibly the most intelligent and competent person I have ever met. I have known quite a number of brilliant people. Be that as it may, my mentee had long greasy hair and dressed like a homeless person. When people got to know him they generally liked and respected him. The problem was that he didn't wear the costume. Since he did not wear business casual attire and cut his hair; the public, his bosses and his peers gave him no respect. Even though he was often correct he was considered a joke. His supervisor told me that if I couldn't "straighten him out" in out in two weeks he was fired.

I spent quite a bit of time talking with him about why he wanted this job and how it fit into his ultimate goals. With one week to go he decided that he would try a new costume and a haircut. He asked me to help him pick out the costumes.

Over the weekend we went shopping and in the end he looked so good you would have thought he was Brad Pitt's younger brother. I could barely recognize him.

Monday morning a new employee arrived at work. He played and worked well with others and within months was promoted. Four years later he left the company and started his own. I caught a glimpse of him on the local news and he is a man who commands respect. The only difference between him now and before was that he has mastered his craft and he looks the part.

When I was 22 years old I was a substitute teacher with a very young face. I looked like a middle school student. However when I put on a shirt with a collar, a tie and a pair of Italian loafers; I became the intriguing young man who had something to say. High school children were spellbound. Teaching peers showed respect for me and administrators were supportive of my goal to being a teacher.

Costuming is not only fun but can be an effective tool for getting others to be supportive and programing your mind (your thinking and feeling).

The important thing is that you make your goal tangible.

Principle #3 Make a Plan and write it down.

Making a concrete plan and writing it down is crucial. The plan you write down should be, what has to happen and in what order, in order to achieve your final outcome. If you draw or write out your steps to your final goal you will be very clear in how to get to your final goal. When you don't know how to do something in your plan; you should include where can you learn to do it or who can you hire to do that segment.

I have always figured I can rent the services of a person if I don't Know how to do it. Most people with specialized competencies or a Doctorate can had for $100 cash an hour.

Twenty hours of forty hours into my flight training I realized that it would cost me thousands of dollars a year to keep my own plane and fly it. Then I had a flash of insight. I could rent a plane and instructor any time I want and it will only cost a few hundred dollars a year. I can go mountain flying or night flying or just go for a spin around the airport anytime I want. I don't need a pilot's license just a pilot!!

So don't let a lack of knowledge or skill keep you for attaining your goals. Think outside the box.

The path to a goal can often be strewn with numerous detours and barriers. Identifying these hazards can be difficult in the fog that comes from fighting to achieve your goal.

For example, a young women or man can be distracted from their goals in education simply by following their basic need for love and belonging. If they give into this impulse they may end up in all manner of trouble that will make their goals more difficult or impossible.

An unplanned pregnancy in college can really distract from the goal of graduating. If one doesn't have a clear list of objectives needed to get to the final outcome; a person may take another path leading to an unintended outcome.

An Odd but True Story

At the local state college there are some young women who have the goal of graduation clearly in their minds. They want to graduate and they have actually coined a term. They call themselves S.L.U.G. (Student Lesbians Until Graduated). While this is obviously an extremely reactive strategy to the issue; it does speak about some women who have goals and don't want to be distracted from their goals by men. I would perhaps suggest a less extreme strategy. Perhaps abstinence from sexual intercourse would be adequate to remedy this issue.

Here are some more examples of people I have known that did not have a clear plan for their goal achievement. They really messed up because they did have a clear enough plan. If they had a concrete step by step plan the might not have had major trouble.

I'll never forget a friend who was accepted in the Washington State Patrol training program. On the night of his acceptance he went out to celebrate. Six hours later he called from the local jail. He had been stopped for driving drunk and arrested for fighting with the police. He clearly didn't have a clear plan for his career path. He was later rejected from the teaching profession because of his criminal history. He generally wasn't even a drinker.

A counselor I know took a client in her own vehicle to do some shopping. The client falsely claimed sexual abuse. Even though she was eventually cleared of the allegations; her malpractice insurance, and government employment have been nearly impossible to maintain.

An acquaintance Studied for four years to get an Engineering degree. She spent the whole four years mildly stoned and studying. There is a test some Engineers have to take to become a Licensed Civil Engineer. She could not pass it unless she was stoned and most employers nowadays test for drugs. She failed the both test several times and was forced to take a job in a bakery.

There are detours that are fair and unfair in the game of life. A person needs to really think over their every move and check if it is in alignment with their plan for their goals.

Principle number #4 Celebrate wins.

When you conquer an objective on your way to a goal celebrate. Do just say yippee! Do something like throw a party and sing songs and be happy. Refresh yourself and get ready for the next accomplishment. Create a ritual and live it up.

My modest celebration is to always go eat Chinese food when I finish a term in school or get a new job or achieved some other hard fought goal. In the past I would eat two plates of fried shrimp! To this day I still eat ½ a dozen shrimp when I achieve a goal. Eating two dozen fried shrimp does not fit well my goal of physical fitness and wellness.

When you have concrete goal and plan all of a sudden it is easier to make those smaller choices. Those small behaviors either support your achievement or distract.

How big of a hole in a rowboat does it take to sink it? The answer is that any hole will sink the boat given enough time.

Looking for Holes

I called this process of accessing your status as you are on your path toward your goal "cleaning up." We must intermittently check to make sure that every area of our lives makes sense. For example, if I say I want to weigh 185 pounds but I guzzle sugar soda pops daily; am I going to make my goal? No. No matter how much time spend at the gym I never make my goal.

I recently heard on a talk show that some women and men are lean and light and in the gym 7 days week. Then drink and eat until they throw up 5-6 nights a week. The upshot has been organ damage and bone fractures because of poor nutrition. It turns out you cannot really have your cake and eat it too.

All these examples seem obvious to us but in the fog that happens when you battle for a goal, things can get murky. People make these bonehead mistakes because they are not cautiously guarding there goals.

Principle # 5 Think inside and outside the box

Stay on your path (inside the box) but also be willing to entertain wild card ideas. Is there another way? Who does this other way? Where else can I work on this goal? How else can I achieve this goal? Is there a better goal or a bigger goal? Is there another way around this problem?

In order to illustrate how to think outside the box I will give you some real life examples. These are just a few selected out 100 examples that I or my friends have done.

Problem: I had no money to get my Special Education endorsement.

Answer: I applied for an obscure government program that paid for everything.

Six days later I had a check that paid for it all.

Problem: A friend wanted to become a scuba instructor and he had no money.

Answer: He borrowed money for plane ticket from me and worked in a scuba school in Thailand. He became an intern and lived for free while he stacked up a bunch of scuba instructor certifications. A year later he paid me back and continued his underwater career in the South China Sea.

Problem: I wanted to do Peace Corps but didn't want to give two years.

Answer: I got a friend to start a program for US Public Health service. I was the first participant.

Problem: I wanted to do a resident camp job but only part time in the summer.

Answer: I was the first director of an English/Chinese language camp held at the University of Washington campus 1992-1994

Problem: I didn't speak Chinese

Answer: I hired undergraduate language students as staff at my camp.

Problem: I wanted to spend a month in Mexico really talking to people and learning Spanish.

Answer: I became a missionary for a Christian church and opened up a mothballed mission station in a barrio in Tijuana Mexico.

Problem: I Needed a Job and wasn't invited for an interview at a local high school.

Answer: I drove to the interviews and knocked on the principal's window. I was hired on the spot and worked there for four years.

Problem: I wanted to be a Counselor in an alternative high school but they weren't hiring at the time.

Answer: Went to the local alternative school without an appointment for an informational interview and had the job a few hours later.

Summary

It takes a certain amount of guts to think outside the box and sometimes it doesn't work out. However if you sit around waiting for something to come your way; you may wait for the rest of your life. I would caution you again. Be careful what you want because if you have a plan and or think outside the box you may get what you are seeking.

An Example

When I was a very young man, I convinced a HR director to hire me for a book keeping job. After three mind numbing hours I went to lunch and never returned. I called them back and explained that the terms of employment were excellent but that the job was not what I expected. I do my homework before I make any move toward any goal nowadays.

Principle #6 Surround, Yourself with Support

Life in general, and goal achievement specifically, is much easier when you surround yourself with supportive people. To have supportive people in your life, you must be supportive to others. Without enabling irresponsible behavior, be generous and thoughtful. People whom you have helped out are much more likely to help you. Don't count things out and try to balance things out tit for tat. Just give and be thoughtful. Make it a habit to be kind and courteous. It really makes it possible for everyone to have fun.

One time I bought two cheap fans for my home. Then I realized that the secretaries at work were suffering from a lack of air conditioning during a heat wave. So since the fans where not needed imminently at home, I loaned them to the secretaries. It turned out that one of the fans was missing a part. However, the maintenance man manufactured a substitute part and the fans worked out great at work and at home. What goes around tends to come around.

Another time I went to work and noticed that the office staff was suffering from cold. The heat was out and it was barely above freezing. I went back to my car trunk and loaned hats and coats to everybody that needed them. Later in the spring it went to 104 degrees inside my classroom. We had to evacuate but it was very touching to see how the secretaries and the maintenance man were attentive to my heating problem. It was almost fun to have the problem.

Besides we spend a full 1/3 of our days in the work environment, we should try to make as pleasant for each other as possible.

Principle #7 Live the dream.

This is not just sage advice. It is your reward for hard work. Let other people give you recognition. This is a rare thing these days. If you get a certificate or award put it on your wall. I have a large collection of awards and certificates in a special corner in my home. It reminds me of what I have achieved. Believe it or not over time you will tend to forget the things that meant so much, long ago.

Baby Steps

Part of the art of goal setting and achieving is finding a way to feel good about the whole process. One way to get in the whole positive mindset is to purposely view every baby step as a necessary and important little achievement worthy of being celebrated. Then you will find yourself celebrating all the time. As a celebrating, happy person, you will find the burdens of daily struggle much lighter.

An Optimist

For years I have practiced celebrating the little wins in life. People have consistently called me an optimist. I am not an optimist with my head in the clouds. I am an optimistic with my feet firmly planted on the little wins in life as I work my way towards my goals. It is easier to be a happy optimist when you concretely see progress.

Principle #8 Facing Non-achievement

One should courageously face up to non-achievement. Non-achievement is quite different from failure. Non-achievement is the fact that a goal was not met. It can be caused by mistakes you have made or factors out of your control. There is no blame or shame in non-achievement. It is said that Thomas Edison made nearly 1000 attempts to produce a working light bulb, before he got it right. He never saw these attempts as failures. He just felt it was part of the process of searching for an answer to his goal.

If he had given up he would have been a failure. Failure is giving up. In our culture and language we have used the word "failure" to mean "non-achievement" but they are two very different things. We can always control our status as a failure by our attitude. How we answer the question, "Have we given up on the goal?" determines if we are a failure.

I can only think of one thing in my life in which I was a failure. When I directed a Chinese/English Language program, it was a given that I would learn a modest amount of Chinese. I tried on and off for three years and did not learn even a little bit. The language is tonal and I just could not hear the tones. There is a physical reason for which I had difficulty, but it is really just an excuse. I did not do the things that where needed to learn the language. I failed. I gave up.

When I attempted graduate school the first time, I did not fail because it was just a stepping stone to another graduate program. I did not give up. I just used a different strategy and was rewarded with Master's in Counseling and Community Psychology plus a School Counseling certification. My first try at graduate school was only six months. I did very well but decided I wanted another kind of program in another school. It was not wasted time or money. It helped me get a better view of my goal.

Principle #9 Keep your life in balance

This is an area which I find challenging. While most people seem to have trouble dedicating, themselves to hard work; I have trouble dedicating myself to rest and relaxation. Unlike a friend I have, whom just doesn't feel worthy of rest and relaxation; I feel I deserve to rest. I just often have trouble sitting around. It is kind of like a sports car shifting from fifth gear to second gear on the freeway. It is mildly traumatic for me sit and do nothing. Just last month I took a two week vacation and decided I would rest and watch TV.

Fourteen days later I had completed and published three more short stories/books on Amazon.com. I didn't even notice I was working! Writing is pure joy for me. Still if I don't find ways to relax and recreate I will have an early death.

We should just schedule down time and enjoy it. Recreation puts us back together after all the stress a strain. Here is an analogy. When a weight lifter does her workout it tears down muscle fibers. It is the resting of the muscles in the off days that the muscles get stronger. Once we see that down time is productive it will be much easier to rest. A balanced life is critical in the long run.

Self-image as a Person Seeking a Goal

Unless you risk it by taking chances, a solid sense of self and self-esteem do not get a chance to form. For example when I began write short titles for Amazon.com my tension was extreme. I didn't have a sense of my competence as a writer. I was terribly worried that what I had to offer wasn't good enough.

Indeed as it turned out some people really didn't like some of my work and said so rather harshly. This forced me to evaluate my work. I carefully went back and read what I had produced. In spite of the harsh review of "A little Benedictine Oblate Manual" I decided that the reviewer had not actually read the book carefully. The book was good and another reviewer said so.

The point is that I had to come to terms with my own self-image. I finally concluded that I was a good beginning writer and my work was worth reading. If I had decided otherwise it just would have meant that I had to keep working to improve, which what I do anyway. I have learned a lot about writing in the last year and I am even more polished in this my 26th short work! It is in the stretching and straining to write better, and the reflecting in between sessions that I gain strength as a writer and a person.

Conclusion

We can set goals and make our way like a sailboat at sea, or we can drift around like a log in the bay. There are some things to be said for just drifting through life. We can blame everything that befalls us on someone or something else! We can take life as it happens to us. We can take no real responsibility. Many people do this and it works for them.

I preferred to set goals and then enjoy the ride. I take full responsibility for my life and the things I do. Much to the irritation of the drifters I have fun living out somewhere on the edge. But I am not reckless. I do my homework and talk to experts before I set a prudent goal. Then with a gleeful attitude I work my way toward my goals.

I would estimate that ninety nine out of one hundred goals which I have sought came true in my life so far. Perhaps the percentage is even higher. All I know is that we all have a limited time on the earth and we will use that time one way or another. I just enjoy setting and achieving goals. It is the thrill of risk taking I enjoy. It is the thrill of living a life designed around my interests.

How to Become an Achiever

I would set small goals at first so that you are almost guaranteed success. Follow the above principles and then reflect upon how it goes. After you get comfortable with success, the sky is the limit. Dare to dream big and then start building a plan for achieving.

Best Regards December 30, 2013

Other Books by James Nugent

How I Sailed From Olympia to the San Juan Islands, and Returned Safely

An Alternative Boating Guide to Southern Puget Sound

How and Why I lived Aboard

Kayaking Budd Inlet in South Puget Sound

I Speak Esperanto

The Rainbow Road and Other Signs of God's Love

Living an Abundant Life, Within Your Means

Social Jujitsu and Powerful Principles for Managing Social Conflict

Blackjack on My Small Budget

A Little Benedictine Oblate Manuel

Without Speech

All things work

Loving Time with Your Creator

Personal Adventures in a Life of Learning

The Good News about Being Catholic

E-book Writing and Overcoming Barriers to Creativity

E-book Writing and Organizing Your Ideas

My Forty Days for Life 2013

Lifestyle Reality Observing

How to Sail in the Winter

How to Get Your Kid to Move Out

How to Get What Want

Sex, Abstinence, and Happiness

Cynthia Says Radio Show – Anger is a choice

Available at Amazon.com in Kindle E-Book and or Audible Book or Paperback

Reflections and Notes

www.ingramcontent.com/pod-product-compliance
Lightning Source LLC
Chambersburg PA
CBHW060352290526
45791CB00004B/1644